TODAY'S ★ ★ ★ ★ ★
COAST GUARD
HEROES

by Joyce Markovics

Consultant: Fred Pushies
U.S. SOF Adviser

BEARPORT
PUBLISHING

New York, New York

Credits

Cover and Title Page, © U.S. Coast Guard/Petty Officer First Class CC Clayton and © Science Faction/ SuperStock; 4, © AP Photo/John Bazemore; 5, © Science Faction/SuperStock; 6T, © ZUMA Press/Newscom; 6B, © U.S. Coast Guard/Petty Officer Eric J. Chandler; 7, © ZUMA Press/Newscom; 8T, U.S. Coast Guard/ Petty Officer 3rd Class Etta Smith; 8B, © AP Photo/David J. Phillip; 9L, © AP Photo/Robert Galbraith; 9R, © U.S. Coast Guard/Petty Officer 3rd Class Etta Smith; 10T, © Benjamin Lowy/Getty Images; 10B, © U.S. Coast Guard; 11, © U.S. Coast Guard/Petty Officer 2nd Class Bill Colclough; 12T, © U.S. Coast Guard; 12B, © Jason Murray/A-Frame/ZUMA Press/Newscom; 13, © U.S. Coast Guard; 14T, © U.S. Coast Guard/Petty Officer Pamela J. Manns; 14B, © Hoberman Collection/SuperStock; 15, © U.S. Navy/Photographer's Mate 2nd Class Eli J. Medellin; 16, © U.S. Coast Guard; 17, © U.S. Coast Guard/Petty Officer Pamela J. Manns; 18T, © U.S. Department of Defense/Samantha L. Quigley; 18B, © Bjørn Ottosen/www.maritimephoto.no; 19, © U.S. Air Force/Scott H. Spitzer; 20T, Illustration by Kim Jones; 20B, © David C. Rehner/Shutterstock; 21, © U.S. Coast Guard; 22T, © U.S. Coast Guard/PA3 Mike Hvozda; 22B, © U.S. Coast Guard/PA2 Tom Sperduto; 23, © Spencer Platt/Getty Images; 24, © U.S. Coast Guard/Chief Brandon Brewer; 25, © Robert Rosamilio/NY Daily News Archive via Getty Images; 26T, © U.S. Coast Guard/PA1 Tom Sperduto; 26B, © U.S. Navy/Petty Officer 2nd Class Jason Zalasky; 27, © U.S. Department of Defense; 28, © U.S. Coast Guard; 29T, © U.S. Coast Guard/Petty Officer 1st Class Anastasia Devlin; 29B, © U.S. Coast Guard; 31, © Karl R. Martin/Shutterstock.

Publisher: Kenn Goin
Senior Editor: Lisa Wiseman
Creative Director: Spencer Brinker
Design: Dawn Beard Creative
Photo Researcher: Picture Perfect Professionals, LLC

Library of Congress Cataloging-in-Publication Data

Markovics, Joyce L.
  Today's Coast Guard heroes / by Joyce Markovics.
     p. cm. — (Acts of courage: inside America's military)
  Includes bibliographical references and index.
  Audience: Ages 7-12.
  ISBN-13: 978-1-61772-448-0 (library binding)
  ISBN-10: 1-61772-448-3 (library binding)
  1. United States. Coast Guard—Search and rescue operations—Juvenile literature. 2. United States. Coast Guard—Biography—Juvenile literature. 3. Heroes—United States—Juvenile literature. I. Title.
  VG53.M376 2012
  363.28'6092273—dc23
                              2011043245

For more information, write to Bearport Publishing Company, Inc., 45 West 21st Street, Suite 3B, New York, New York 10010. Printed in the United States of America.

10 9 8 7 6 5 4 3 2 1

★ ★ ★ Contents ★ ★ ★

Always Ready

The three-person **crew** of the fishing boat *Mary Lynn* was in serious trouble on August 26, 2005. They were trapped in the Gulf of Mexico by a fierce storm. Towering 40-foot (12-m) waves had slammed into the boat, knocking the crew into the water. Under a pitch-black sky, they clung to the back of the boat, hoping that the sea would not drag them under. Luckily, the U.S. Coast Guard was on its way.

The storm on August 26, 2005, caused dangerous conditions for people in the Gulf of Mexico.

Before the crew was thrown into the water by the high waves, they were able to send out an emergency signal to the Coast Guard.

One of the five branches of the **armed forces**, the U.S. Coast Guard was established in 1790—more than 200 years ago. Since then, the Coast Guard has courageously protected the nation's waters from **terrorist** attacks and other dangerous situations. One of the Coast Guard's most important jobs, however, is to save people who are in danger in the water—like the crew of the *Mary Lynn*.

The U.S. Coast Guard also protects the nation's waterways by searching boats for drugs and other illegal goods.

The members of the U.S. Coast Guard work in many places in the United States and around the world. The parts of this map that are highlighted in red show where some of the events in this book took place.

A Killer Storm

Kenyon Bolton

Rank:	Aviation Survival Technician Third Class
Hometown:	Clearwater, Florida
Event:	Hurricane Katrina
Date:	August 26–27, 2005
Honor:	Distinguished Flying Cross

As crew members of the *Mary Lynn* hung on to the back of their boat, Coast Guard **rescue swimmer** Kenyon Bolton was lowered by his team from a **Jayhawk helicopter** into the Gulf of Mexico. Waves pounded his body as he fought to reach the *Mary Lynn*'s crew members. When he finally reached them, he felt something brush between his legs. It was a shark! "I was surprised it was so close to the surface in such rough weather," said Bolton. "It made me think twice about what was out of sight." Fortunately, the shark quickly swam away.

When there are stormy seas, rescuers face great danger from huge waves and strong winds.

Bolton then attached a **rescue cable** to each of the *Mary Lynn*'s crew members, one at a time. The helicopter team **hoisted** them out of the raging waters and into the helicopter—saving their lives. "They were all exhausted," Bolton said. "They'd been through a long night of giant waves and stress."

The storm that slammed the crew of the *Mary Lynn* was **Hurricane** Katrina. Over the following days, it grew larger and stronger. When it hit land in Louisiana on August 29, 2005, the brave members of the U.S. Coast Guard rescued nearly 33,000 people!

For his bravery, Coast Guard rescue swimmer Kenyon Bolton (right) was awarded the Distinguished Flying Cross during a ceremony on January 27, 2006. The medal is awarded to members of the armed forces for extraordinary heroism while in flight.

Helicopter Help

Jason Dorval

Rank:	Lieutenant
Home State:	New York
Event:	Hurricane Katrina
Date:	August 29–September 6, 2005
Honor:	Distinguished Flying Cross

On August 29, 2005, Hurricane Katrina unleashed its fury on New Orleans, flooding much of the city. "If there was ever a Coast Guard war zone, that would be downtown New Orleans those first nights," remembered Lieutenant Jason Dorval, a Coast Guard helicopter pilot.

Many people who were unable to leave their homes before the storm became trapped by the floodwaters and were left stranded on their rooftops.

On August 30, Dorval and his team flew over the eastern part of the city, searching for stranded people. "All the houses were flooded and people were waving flashlights off the roofs . . . there's just hundreds, thousands of these lights," said Dorval. From the helicopter, Dorval's crew lowered a rescue swimmer in a special basket to the people on the roofs below. Then the swimmer helped each person get into the basket so that it could be lifted back into the helicopter. "We'd move house to house," Dorval recalled. "The **motivation** that kept me going was that there were always more people to be saved out there."

A man stranded by Hurricane Katrina is hoisted into a Coast Guard helicopter in a rescue basket.

With the help of his crew, Dorval rescued 40 patients from a flooded hospital on the evening of September 1.

Lieutenant Jason Dorval won a Distinguished Flying Cross for rescuing more than 330 people in the days following Hurricane Katrina.

Deepwater Disaster

Kurt Peterson

Rank:	Chief Aviation Survival Technician
Event:	Deepwater Horizon oil rig explosion
Date:	April 20, 2010
Honors:	Sikorsky Humanitarian Service Award and the Association for Rescue at Sea (AFRAS) Vice Admiral Thomas R. Sargent Gold Medal

The U.S. Coast Guard responded to another enormous disaster in 2010—an oil spill in the Gulf of Mexico. The accident took place when the Deepwater Horizon **oil rig** exploded, **spewing** millions of gallons of oil into the Gulf. Flames from the explosion shot 600 feet (183 m) into the air, lighting up the night sky. A Coast Guard helicopter carrying 39-year-old rescue swimmer Kurt Peterson and his team was one of the first on the scene.

Eleven people were immediately killed in the Deepwater Horizon explosion. The injured survivors had severe burns, cuts, and broken bones.

The helicopter circled the fiery rig and then hovered above a nearby supply boat where seriously injured rig workers waited to be taken to the hospital. To reach the victims, Peterson's team lowered him down to the boat using a rescue cable. Peterson braved flying **debris** from the burning oil rig as he carefully loaded each of the injured into a rescue basket, one at a time. Then, they were hoisted up in the basket to the helicopter and flown to the hospital.

Kurt Peterson and his Coast Guard team worked throughout the night to help as many survivors as possible. When thinking back to that day, he remembered: "The whole crew, without them I couldn't have done any of it."

Kurt Peterson received the AFRAS award on September 22, 2011. This award is given to members of the Coast Guard who have shown extraordinary bravery during a rescue at sea. He also received the Sikorsky Humanitarian Service Award in March 2011, which honors those who save lives, protect property, and help those in need through helicopter rescue.

Bold and Brave

Randall Black

Rank: Lieutenant

Event: Plane crash

Date: January 29, 2009

Honor: 2010 Department of Defense African American History Month Recognition Award and Elmer Stone Rescue Award

When disaster strikes, the Coast Guard is often the first rescue team on the scene. On January 29, 2009, a pilot was sightseeing in his plane off Half Moon Bay in California when the engine suddenly died. The pilot had no choice but to crash-land the plane into the ice-cold waters of the Pacific Ocean.

This photo shows Half Moon Bay, where the pilot crash-landed his plane.

Fortunately, Coast Guard pilot Randall Black and his seven-person crew were flying in a plane nearby. Black spotted the injured pilot holding on to a wing of the downed plane. He knew that the pilot could freeze in the icy water if he didn't act quickly. Black steered his plane so that it was directly above the crash, and then told his crew to drop a **life raft** to the pilot. The pilot swam to the raft and was later rescued by a helicopter. Had it not been for Black's fast response and bravery, the pilot could have died in the water.

The plane shown here is similar to the one Pilot Randall Black used in the January 2009 rescue. In February 2010, he was honored with the African American History Month Recognition Award in Atlanta, Georgia, for his bravery during the rescue. He also received the Elmer Stone Rescue Award for showing exceptional performance during a rescue.

Members of the U.S. Coast Guard are sometimes called **Guardians** or Coasties.

Capsized!

Kristin Reger Lunkley

Rank:	Petty Officer
Hometown:	McAllen, Texas
Event:	Overturned sailboat
Date:	July 24, 2008
Honor:	Coast Guard Medal

It's the team effort that makes many Coast Guard rescue missions successful. On July 24, 2008, a sailboat, named *Wing It*, **capsized** near the Golden Gate Bridge in San Francisco Bay. When the boat flipped over, the man sailing it was trapped underneath. A Guardian saw the accident happen from a nearby Coast Guard station. He alerted his lifeboat rescue team, which included Petty Officer Kristin Reger Lunkley. The team got into their boat and headed out to the *Wing It*. When they were near the upside-down boat, Lunkley attached a **lifeline** to herself and then dove into the chilly water.

San Francisco Bay in California is a popular area for sailing.

The sailboat was drifting dangerously close to some jagged rocks. Battling four-foot (1-m) waves, Lunkley swam as fast as she could to the overturned boat. Reaching the man underneath it, however, wouldn't be easy.

A Motor Life Boat

The Coast Guard uses special boats called MLBs (Motor Life Boats) for rescue **missions** at sea. The boats are strong and fast. They are designed to return to an upright position in only ten seconds if they are knocked over by a large wave.

Another Life Saved

Without hesitation, Lunkley untied the lifeline that connected her to the Coast Guard boat. She attached it to an extra **life jacket** that she had brought with her. Then she pushed the life jacket under the capsized boat. She instructed the trapped man to put it on. After he did, Lunkley yanked the lifeline with all her might to pull the man out from under the boat. However, the man's foot became tangled in some ropes attached to the sail. Lunkley acted quickly and cut the ropes. She then gave the lifeline another tug, finally freeing the man from under the boat. He was then picked out of the water by Lunkley's Coast Guard team.

The capsized
Wing It

The man caught underneath the sailboat was trapped in the **cabin**, where he had just enough room to keep his head above water.

For risking her life to save the trapped sailor, Lunkley was awarded the Coast Guard Medal. "I feel honored to receive this award, but it really belongs to the whole crew," said Lunkley. "We were a team out there."

Petty Officer Kristin Reger Lunkley was 29 years old when she was awarded the Coast Guard Medal on December 8, 2010. This medal is given to Guardians who have shown extreme heroism by putting themselves in danger to save lives.

Tanker Explosion

Zee O. Lee

Rank:	Aviation Survival Technician Third Class
Home State:	New Jersey
Event:	Tanker Explosion
Date:	February 28, 2004
Honor:	Coast Guard Medal and USO Service Hero of the Year Award

When a person is in danger, Guardians are always willing to risk their own safety to save a life. For example, in the winter of 2004, the 570-foot (174-m) **tanker** *Bow Mariner* caught fire and exploded 50 miles (80 km) off the coast of Virginia. The ship was carrying millions of gallons of **ethanol** and a full tank of **fuel oil**, which spilled into the ocean. Fortunately, a Coast Guard rescue helicopter received the emergency call and rushed to help.

The *Bow Mariner* tanker before the explosion

When the helicopter arrived, the Coast Guard team saw a member of the tanker's crew in the water. Without hesitation, rescue swimmer Zee O. Lee asked to be lowered from the helicopter into the freezing, **polluted** water to save the victim. Once in the water, wearing only a **wet suit** to protect him from the deadly chemicals, he swam to the tanker's crew member. The chemicals in the water burned Lee's eyes, but he pushed on. Once he reached the victim, Lee placed himself and the man in a special rescue **sling**. Then they were both hoisted up to the helicopter. Once inside, Lee immediately gave the man **CPR**. "A few times, he simply stopped breathing," said Lee. However, Lee kept him alive until he was taken to a hospital.

Guardians are taught first aid and CPR to care for people who are ill or injured.

Zee O. Lee, shown here being lowered from a Coast Guard helicopter during training, was awarded the Coast Guard Medal on September 13, 2004. For his heroic actions, he also received the USO Service Hero of the Year Award in September 2005.

A Lake Rescue

Steven M. Ruh

Rank: Boatswain's Mate Third Class (Later promoted to Commander)

Hometown: Hamburg, New York

Event: Lake Ontario rescue

Date: August 15, 2006

Honor: Coast Guard Medal

In addition to its work at sea, the Coast Guard **patrols** the country's many lakes. On August 15, 2006, an emergency call came in at Coast Guard Station Oswego in upstate New York. An 18-year-old woman was walking along the steep, rocky shore of Lake Ontario when a large wave swept her into the lake's rough waters. Boatswain's Mate Steven M. Ruh and his team responded to the call in a Coast Guard lifeboat.

Lake Ontario

When Ruh and his team arrived on the scene, they found the woman clinging to a rope at the base of a cliff as eight-to-ten-foot (2-to-3-m) waves struck her. Firefighters had lowered down the rope and unsuccessfully tried to save her by pulling her up the cliff. Ruh attached a lifeline to himself and plunged into the water. He swam more than 100 yards (91 m) to reach the woman and then placed his body between her and the jagged rocks. He fought to keep his head above water while he put the woman in a life jacket. As the Coast Guard team used the lifeline to pull Ruh and the woman to safety in the stormy waters, Ruh was dragged underwater. Still, he managed to save the woman and himself. Ruh remembers that day as being "exhausting but incredibly rewarding."

Members of the Coast Guard often use lifelines, such as this one, during water rescues.

Steven Ruh was awarded the Coast Guard Medal for his heroism on August 15, 2006.

The woman Ruh saved had a broken leg and severe cuts. She was immediately taken to the hospital after her rescue and later recovered from her injuries.

Under Attack

Carlos Perez

Rank: Petty Officer Third Class (Later promoted to Maritime Enforcement Specialist)

Hometown: Brooklyn, New York

Event: Terrorist attack on New York City

Date: September 11, 2001

Coast Guard heroes also helped rescue people in New York City on September 11, 2001. On that bright, sunny morning, Petty Officer Carlos Perez received an emergency call that an airplane had struck the North Tower of the World Trade Center. At the time, Perez was on a boat patrolling New York Harbor. He and his team immediately headed to lower Manhattan. "Our crew responded to the first crash, treating it as if it were an accident," recalled Perez.

A Coast Guard boat rushes to downtown Manhattan on September 11, 2001.

"As we approached lower Manhattan . . . the second plane made its way in and crashed into the second tower right above our heads," said Perez. Fierce flames and smoke filled the sky. Within two hours, the giant towers tumbled to the ground.

The North and South Towers, called the twin towers, after being hit on September 11, 2001

On September 11, 2001, terrorists **hijacked** four airplanes full of people. They flew two planes into the World Trade Center in New York City. They crashed another one into the **Pentagon** in Virginia, and one crashed into a field in Pennsylvania. About 3,000 people were killed.

A Huge Evacuation

Thick smoke, dust, and debris blanketed downtown Manhattan. Thousands of people rushed out of nearby office buildings and gathered along the waterfront. The Coast Guard radioed all available boats in the harbor to help **evacuate** people. Then Guardians loaded thousands onto the boats, which took them to safe areas nearby, such as New Jersey. They also helped direct the jumble of boat traffic going in and out of New York Harbor.

People waiting anxiously to leave lower Manhattan after the attacks

The evacuations took place throughout the day. By 3:00 p.m., most of downtown Manhattan had been emptied. "All in all, I think that everyone served honorably and did all that was required of them to restore order and safety. For what it's worth, and what we faced, we did it right that day," said Perez.

On September 11, the Coast Guard coordinated one of the largest rescues in U.S. history. They successfully evacuated between 300,000 and 500,000 people that day.

Coast Guard boats and a variety of other small boats, such as ferries and tugboats, were used to evacuate people from New York City on September 11, 2001.

Serving Overseas

Holly Harrison

Rank: Lieutenant Commander
Hometown: Tucson, Arizona
Conflict: Iraq War
Date: March 22, 2003
Honor: Bronze Star

The Coast Guard also assists with war efforts around the world. When the United States invaded Iraq in 2003, some Guardians were sent there to patrol Iraq's coast. Lieutenant Commander Holly Harrison captained the 110-foot (33-m) **cutter** *Aquidneck*. She and her team searched Iraqi boats for weapons that might be used to harm U.S. troops, and protected Iraqi shorelines from terrorist attacks.

Arctic Ocean
ASIA
NORTH AMERICA
EUROPE
Iraq
Atlantic Ocean
AFRICA
Pacific Ocean
Pacific Ocean
SOUTH AMERICA
Indian Ocean
AUSTRALIA
Southern Ocean

The Aquidneck

Iraq is a country in the Middle East that the United States went to war with in 2003. Some U.S. government officials believed that Saddam Hussein, the ruler of Iraq, was trying to build dangerous weapons to use against the United States and other countries. Though these weapons were never found, the United States and its **allies** were able to remove Hussein from power.

One of Harrison's most dangerous missions took place on March 22, 2003. Her job was to **escort** special boats that were looking for floating **mines**, which the enemy had placed in the water to destroy U.S. ships. To protect the boats looking for mines from terrorist attacks, Harrison and her team moved ahead of them in their cutter in areas that had not yet been cleared of mines. Even though she knew that her boat could be completely torn apart by these bombs, Harrison still steered ahead of the other boats. After a tense mission, she successfully led everyone to safety.

Harrison is one of many brave Guardians who are always ready to serve and to protect the people of the United States. At home and **overseas**, the U.S. Coast Guard has one of the most important jobs in the world—to save lives.

Holly Harrison, the first woman to command a Coast Guard vessel in a combat zone, received a Bronze Star in 2003 for her bravery and leadership as the commander of the *Aquidneck* in Iraq.

More Coast Guard Heroes

Here are a few more members of the U.S. Coast Guard who have worked hard to serve their country.

⭐ Petty Officer Second Class Bonnie Wysocki ⭐

Coast Guard Petty Officer Second Class Bonnie Wysocki spent almost one year in the Middle East working for the Coast Guard's Redeployment Assistance and Inspection Detachment (RAID) team. She worked in Iraq, Afghanistan, and Kuwait, helping the Army inspect and ship supplies and safely transport soldiers to and from the Middle East. For her hard work, Wysocki was honored as one of 18 "Heroes on the Front Lines" by the U.S. government in July 2011.

⭐ Lorrin Ching, Master Electrician ⭐

Lorrin Ching, based in the Hawaiian Islands, is a master electrician for the Coast Guard. In 2009, he started a new energy-saving program for the Coast Guard. He installed energy-efficient lightbulbs and air conditioners that saved energy and cut pollution at several Hawaiian Coast Guard stations. "My field is electricity, and saving it saves money," said Ching. "The less electricity you use, the less pollution you create," he added. "We only have one planet and I am trying to do my part to keep it clean."

Master Electrician Lorrin Ching

⋆ Commander Diane Durham ⋆

On January 12, 2010, an earthquake struck Haiti, destroying much of the city of Port-au-Prince and killing hundreds of thousands of people. Commander Diane Durham immediately sailed her ship, named *Forward*, from Cuba to Haiti to help the Haitian people. *Forward* was the first American ship to arrive in Haiti after the quake. "Everybody in this city (Port-au-Prince) has been hit," said Durham after seeing the damage. Durham and her team helped to direct airplanes into and out of Haiti. Some of the flights carried critically injured people to nearby hospitals. Her team also provided medical supplies, food, and water to the Haitian Coast Guard.

Commander Diane Durham

⋆ Lieutenant Commander Rhonda Fleming-Makell ⋆

In 2002, Lieutenant Commander Rhonda Fleming-Makell started a Coast Guard **canine** unit in the United States—the first of its kind since World War II (1939–1945). The dogs in the unit are specially trained to use their sensitive noses to sniff out explosives in ships and buildings. In March 2004, the dogs discovered bombs and other explosive materials in a house. These could have been used in a terrorist attack against the United States. Thanks to Fleming-Makell's work, the explosives were safely removed and disposed of. "She was instrumental in moving the organization forward and saving lives," said Lieutenant Commander Tracy Slack.

Lieutenant Commander Rhonda Fleming-Makell

Glossary

allies (AL-eyez) friends or supporters

armed forces (ARMD FORSS-IZ) the military groups a country uses to protect itself

cabin (KAB-in) a small room on a ship

canine (KAY-nine) having to do with dogs

capsized (KAP-sized) turned over in the water

CPR (SEE-PEE-AR) letters stand for *cardiopulmonary resuscitation*; a type of rescue in which a person blows air into the mouth and then presses down on the chest of someone whose heart has stopped

crew (KROO) a group of people who work together to get a job done

cutter (KUHT-ur) a small armed boat used by the U.S. military

debris (duh-BREE) scattered pieces of something that has been wrecked or destroyed

escort (ess-KORT) to accompany people in order to protect them

ethanol (ETH-uh-nol) a colorless liquid used to power machines

evacuate (i-VAK-yoo-ate) to move away from a dangerous area

fuel oil (FYOO-uhl OIL) a thick, greasy liquid used to power machines

Guardians (GAR-dee-uhnz) members of the U.S. Coast Guard

hijacked (HYE-jackt) took control of by force

hoisted (HOIS-tid) lifted up

hurricane (HUR-uh-*kane*) a violent storm with very strong, swirling winds

Jayhawk helicopter (JAY-hawk HEL-uh-*kop*-tur) a type of helicopter used by the Coast Guard for search-and-rescue missions

life jacket (LIFE JAK-it) a special vest that keeps people afloat in water

lifeline (LIFE-line) a special rope or line used for saving a life

life raft (LIFE RAFT) an inflatable rubber craft used to rescue people in danger of drowning

mines (MINEZ) bombs placed in the ground or in the water

missions (MISH-uhnz) special jobs

motivation (MOH-tuh-*vay*-shuhn) encouragement to do something

oil rig (OIL RIG) a large platform used as a base for drilling into the sea for oil

overseas (oh-vur-SEEZ) across the ocean

patrols (puh-TROHLZ) watches and protects an area

Pentagon (PEN-tuh-gon) the five-sided building in Virginia that serves as the headquarters of the U.S. Department of Defense

polluted (puh-LOOT-uhd) damaged by harmful waste or chemicals

rescue cable (RESS-kyoo KAY-buhl) a thick wire used to save someone trapped or in danger

rescue swimmer (RESS-kyoo SWIM-ur) a member of the Coast Guard who is trained to rescue people in the water

sling (SLING) a strong loop of cable, chain, or rope used to raise heavy objects

spewing (SPYOO-ing) sending out in great quantity

tanker (TANG-kur) a ship that carries liquids, such as oil

terrorist (TER-ur-ist) a person who uses violence and terror to get what he or she wants

wet suit (WET SOOT) a rubber suit that keeps swimmers warm in cold water

Bibliography

Helvarg, David. *Rescue Warriors: The U.S. Coast Guard, America's Forgotten Heroes.* New York: Thomas Dunne Books (2009).

www.sptimes.com/2005/08/30/Tampabay/Coast_Guard_rescue_cr.shtml

www.uscg.mil/

Read More

Benson, Michael. *The U.S. Coast Guard (U.S. Armed Forces).* Minneapolis, MN: Lerner Publications (2005).

Braulick, Carrie A. *U.S. Coast Guard Cutters.* Mankato, MN: Capstone Press (2007).

David, Jack. *United States Coast Guard.* Minneapolis, MN: Bellwether Media (2008).

Goldish, Meish. *Coast Guard: Civilian to Guardian (Becoming a Soldier).* New York: Bearport Publishing (2011).

Learn More Online

To learn more about today's U.S. Coast Guard heroes, visit
www.bearportpublishing.com/ActsofCourage

Index

About the Author

Joyce Markovics is a writer and editor in New York City. In writing this book, she wished to pay tribute to all the brave men and women who have risked their own safety for the sake of others.